AF426425

JOSEPH'S COLORFUL DREAMS

Bible Bedtime Story

BLUME POTTER

INTRODUCTION

Joseph's Colorful Dreams is more than just a collection of Bible bedtime stories; it's a journey through one of the most inspiring tales from the Bible, thoughtfully crafted to captivate young hearts and minds. This beautifully written series brings the timeless story of Joseph—the boy with the multicolored coat—into the world of your little ones, making the lessons of forgiveness, perseverance, and faith accessible and relatable.

Each chapter of this book is designed to not only entertain but also to instill important values that will stay with your children or grandchildren for a lifetime. As they follow Joseph's incredible journey from the pit to the palace, they'll learn about the power of God's providence, the beauty of forgiveness, and the strength of character that comes from trusting in God's plan.

With its engaging storytelling and charming illustrations, "Joseph's Colorful Dreams" is the perfect addition to your bedtime routine. It's a book that your children or grandchildren will look forward to each night, filling their dreams with hope and love. This is a must-have treasure for any home, creating special moments that you'll cherish forever.

CHAPTER ONE:
THE COAT OF MANY COLORS

Joseph was a young boy who lived with his father, Jacob, and his many brothers in the land of Canaan. Among all his sons, Jacob loved Joseph the most. He was the son of Jacob's old age, and his father's heart was filled with pride and affection for him.

One day, Jacob decided to show his special love for Joseph by giving him a gift—a beautiful coat of many colors. This coat was unlike anything anyone had ever seen. It shimmered with bright reds, deep blues, sunny yellows, and rich greens. When Joseph put on the coat, he felt like the most special person in the world.

Joseph's brothers, however, did not share in his joy. As they watched Joseph twirl around in his colorful coat, their hearts began to fill with jealousy. "Why does Joseph get such a fine coat?" they muttered among themselves. "Does Father love him more than us?"

The jealousy in their hearts grew even stronger when Joseph began to share his dreams with them. "Listen to this dream I had," Joseph told his brothers one morning. "We were all binding sheaves of grain in the field when suddenly, my sheaf stood up straight, and your sheaves gathered around it and bowed down to mine."

His brothers' faces turned sour. "Are you saying you will rule over us?" they snapped. But Joseph, innocent and excited, continued.

A few days later, he had another dream. "I had another dream," Joseph said eagerly. "This time, the sun, the moon, and eleven stars were bowing down to me!"

This was too much for his brothers. Their jealousy turned into resentment. "Who does Joseph think he is?" they grumbled. "First the coat, and now these dreams? Does he think he's better than us?"

The beautiful coat that once filled Joseph with happiness now served as a reminder to his brothers of their father's favoritism and the dreams that made them feel small. Their hearts grew heavy with jealousy, and they began to plot against Joseph, unable to see that his dreams were more than just stories—they were a glimpse into the extraordinary path that lay ahead.

CHAPTER TWO:
BETRAYED BY HIS BROTHERS

The jealousy Joseph's brothers felt only grew stronger with each passing day. They could no longer bear the sight of Joseph in his colorful coat, nor the thought of his dreams that placed him above them. So one day, when Joseph came to check on them in the fields, they saw an opportunity to get rid of him.

"Here comes the dreamer," one brother whispered. "Let's throw him into a pit and say a wild animal attacked him. Then we'll see what comes of his dreams."

The brothers agreed. As soon as Joseph reached them, they grabbed him, tore off his beautiful coat of many colors, and threw him into a deep, dark pit. Joseph cried out for help, but his brothers ignored his pleas.

As they sat down to eat, they noticed a caravan of traders passing by on their way to Egypt. An idea formed in the minds of the brothers. "Why should we leave him in the pit?" one brother said. "Let's sell him to these traders instead. We won't have to shed any blood, and we'll be rid of him for good."

The brothers agreed, and for twenty pieces of silver, they sold Joseph to the traders. As the caravan moved away, taking Joseph with it, the brothers felt a mix of relief and guilt, but they pushed those feelings aside.

To cover their actions, the brothers took Joseph's coat, dipped it in the blood of a goat, and brought it back to their father, Jacob. "We found this," they said, handing him the bloodied coat. "Do you recognize it?"

Jacob's heart broke when he saw the coat. "It is my son's coat!" he cried. "A wild animal has devoured him! Joseph is without doubt torn to pieces." Jacob mourned deeply for his son, refusing to be comforted.

Meanwhile, Joseph was taken far from his home and family, to the land of Egypt. He was sold as a slave to a man named Potiphar, an officer of Pharaoh. Though Joseph was now a slave in a foreign land, far from everything he knew, he held onto his faith. He trusted that God was with him, even in the darkest of times.

CHAPTER THREE: FROM PRISON TO PALACE

In Egypt, Joseph's life was filled with trials. As a slave in Potiphar's house, Joseph worked hard and earned his master's trust. But one day, Potiphar's wife falsely accused Joseph of doing something he didn't do. Without a chance to defend himself, Joseph was thrown into prison.

Even in prison, Joseph did not lose hope. He knew that God was with him, just as He had been all along. Joseph's kind and helpful nature quickly gained him favor with the prison warden, who put him in charge of other prisoners.

One day, two of Pharaoh's servants, the cupbearer and the baker, were thrown into the same prison. Both men had strange dreams that troubled them. When Joseph saw their distress, he asked them about their dreams and, with God's help, he interpreted them.

To the cupbearer, Joseph said, "In three days, Pharaoh will restore you to your position." And to the baker, he said, "In three days, Pharaoh will have you punished." Just as Joseph had said, the dreams came true. The cupbearer was restored to his position, and the baker was punished.

Joseph asked the cupbearer to remember him and mention him to Pharaoh, but the cupbearer forgot about Joseph once he was free.

Two years passed, and Joseph remained in prison. But one night, Pharaoh himself had troubling dreams that no one could interpret. It was then that the cupbearer finally remembered Joseph. He told Pharaoh about the young Hebrew prisoner who had accurately interpreted his dream.

Pharaoh immediately sent for Joseph. When Joseph stood before Pharaoh, he listened carefully to the dreams and, with God's guidance, explained their meaning. "Your dreams, O Pharaoh, mean that Egypt will have seven years of great abundance followed by seven years of severe famine."

Pharaoh was amazed by Joseph's wisdom and the clarity of his interpretation. Recognizing that Joseph had the spirit of

God within him, Pharaoh decided to place him in charge of preparing Egypt for the coming famine. In a remarkable turn of events, Joseph was made a ruler in Egypt, second only to Pharaoh himself.

From a pit to a prison and now to a palace, Joseph's journey was far from ordinary. Yet through every challenge, he remained faithful, trusting that God had a plan for him. Now, dressed not in a coat of many colors but in the robes of Egyptian royalty, Joseph's dreams were beginning to unfold in ways he had never imagined.

CHAPTER FOUR:
A FAMILY REUNION

Many years had passed since Joseph was sold into slavery, and now he was a powerful ruler in Egypt, overseeing the storage and distribution of food during a severe famine. The famine was widespread, affecting many lands, including Canaan, where Joseph's family lived.

Jacob, Joseph's father, heard that there was food in Egypt and sent his sons to buy grain. When they arrived in Egypt, they were brought before Joseph, but they did not recognize him. Joseph, however, knew exactly who they were. The sight of his brothers, the very ones who had betrayed him, stirred many emotions in Joseph. But he kept his identity hidden.

To test their honesty, Joseph accused them of being spies. The brothers, desperate to prove their innocence, explained that they were simply brothers from Canaan, come to buy food. They mentioned their younger brother, Benjamin, still at home with their father. Joseph, wanting to see if they had truly changed, insisted that they bring Benjamin to Egypt.

The brothers returned to Canaan, and after much persuasion, Jacob reluctantly allowed Benjamin to go with them to Egypt. When they returned, Joseph arranged a feast for them but secretly placed a silver cup in Benjamin's sack. After they left, Joseph had them stopped and accused of stealing the cup.

The brothers were terrified, especially when they saw the cup in Benjamin's sack. They begged for mercy, offering themselves as slaves in place of Benjamin, showing Joseph that they were no longer the same men who had sold him into slavery.

Seeing their genuine remorse and love for their youngest brother, Joseph could no longer keep his secret. With tears in his eyes, he revealed his true identity to them. "I am Joseph, your brother, whom you sold into Egypt!" he said.

The brothers were stunned and frightened, fearing that Joseph would seek revenge. But Joseph, with a heart full of forgiveness, told them not to be afraid. "Do not be angry with yourselves for selling me here," he said, "because it was to save lives that God sent me ahead of you."

Joseph's forgiveness was genuine, and he embraced his brothers, weeping with them. It was a moment of reconciliation and healing. Joseph sent them back to Canaan with a message for their father, Jacob, inviting the whole family to come and live in Egypt, where they would be provided for during the remaining years of famine.

Through tears and smiles, the family that had been torn apart by jealousy was now reunited, bound by the threads of forgiveness and love.

CHAPTER FIVE:
FORGIVENESS AND LOVE

Joseph's brothers stood before him, overwhelmed with guilt and fear, but Joseph's heart was filled with compassion. He looked at his brothers, who had once betrayed him, and spoke with kindness and wisdom.

"Do not be afraid," Joseph said gently. "You meant to harm me, but God used it for good. He brought me here so that I could save many lives, including yours. It was all part of His plan."

The brothers were amazed by Joseph's words. They had expected anger and punishment, but instead, they found forgiveness and love. Joseph's heart had been shaped not by bitterness, but by faith in God's purpose.

Joseph invited his brothers to bring their father, Jacob, and all their families to Egypt, where he would take care of them. He sent them back to Canaan with gifts and a message of hope for their father.

When Jacob heard that Joseph was alive and well in Egypt, his heart leaped with joy. He could hardly believe that his beloved son, whom he thought was lost forever, was now a ruler in a foreign land. Jacob and all his family packed up their belongings and made the journey to Egypt.

As Joseph saw his father approaching, he ran to him and embraced him, tears of joy streaming down their faces. The years of separation melted away, and the family was whole once again.

Jacob and his sons settled in Egypt, where they were provided with everything they needed during the years of famine. Joseph's journey, from the pit to the palace, had come full circle. He had been tested, but he had remained faithful, and now he was reunited with his family.

The story of Joseph and his brothers is a powerful reminder of the strength of forgiveness and the beauty of God's plan. What began as a story of jealousy and betrayal ended in love and reconciliation, showing that even in the darkest moments, God is at work, bringing good out of every situation.